The Kottak

Anthropology Atlas

World Countries

The international system includes the political units called "states" or countries as the most important component. The boundaries of countries are the primary source of political division in the world and for most people nationalism is the strongest source of political identity. State boundaries are an important indicator of cultural, linguistic, economic, and other geographic divisions as well, and the states themselves normally serve as the base level for which most global statistics are available. The subfield of geography known as "Political Geography" has as its primary concern the geographic or spatial character of this international system and its components.

Scale: 1 to 122,510,000

Note: All world maps are Robinson projection.

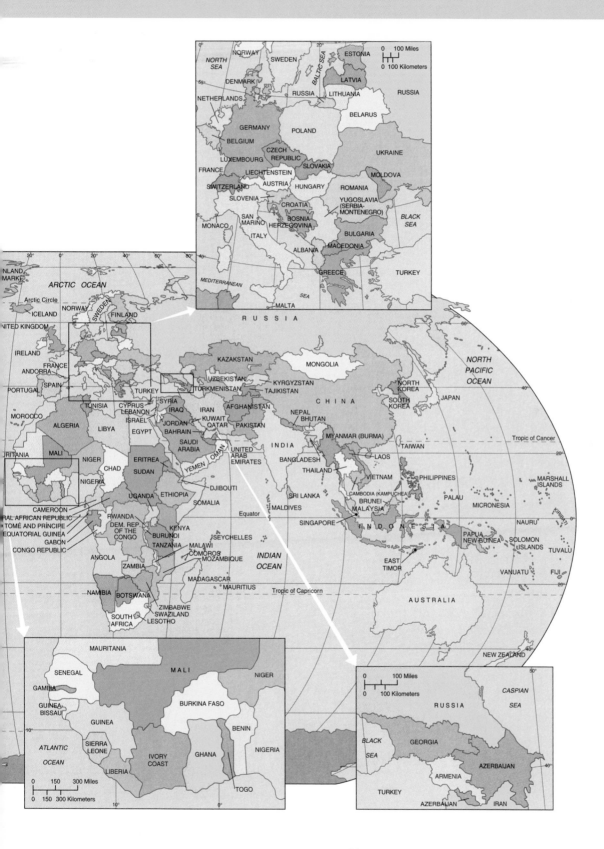

The Kottak

Anthropology Atlas

John L. Allen
University of Wyoming

Audrey C. Shalinsky
University of Wyoming

Boston   Burr Ridge, IL   Dubuque, IA   Madison, WI   New York   San Francisco   St. Louis
Bangkok   Bogotá   Caracas   Lisbon   London   Madrid   Mexico City   Milan   New Delhi
Seoul   Singapore   Sydney   Taipei   Toronto

McGraw-Hill Higher Education ⍟

A Division of The McGraw·Hill Companies

THE KOTTAK ANTHROPOLOGY ATLAS
Published by McGraw-Hill, a business unit of The McGraw-Hill Companies, Inc., 1221 Avenue of the Americas, New York, NY, 10020. Copyright © 2004 by The McGraw-Hill Companies, Inc. All rights reserved. No parts of this publication may be reproduced or distributed in any form or by any means, or stored in a database or retrieval system, without the prior written consent of The McGraw-Hill Companies, Inc., including, but not limited to, in any network or other electronic storage or transmission, or broadcast for distance learning. Some ancillaries, including electronic and printed components, may not be available to customers outside the United States.

This book is printed on acid-free paper

1 2 3 4 5 6 7 8 9 0 DOW/DOW 0 9 8 7 6 5 4 3

ISBN 0-07-283228-2

Publisher: *Phillip A. Butcher*
Sponsoring editor: *Kevin Witt*
Developmental editor: *Pam Gordon*
Marketing manager: *Dan Loch*
Media producer: *Shannon Gattens*
Project manager: *Jean R. Starr*
Production supervisor: *Carol A. Bielski*
Designer: *Cassandra Chu*
Art editor: *Robin Mouat*
Interior design: *Charlie Vitelli*
Typeface: *Optima, ITC-Garamond, and ITC-Garamond Condensed*
Compositor: *McGraw-Hill/Dushkin*
Printer: *R.R. Donnelley/Willard*

Maps reprinted from John L. Allen and Audrey C. Shalinsky, *Student Atlas of Anthropology* (McGraw-Hill, 2004). Copyright ©2004 by the McGraw-Hill Companies, Inc. Reprinted by permission of McGraw-Hill/Dushkin, a division of the McGraw-Hill Companies. All rights reserved.

Library of Congress Cataloging-in-Publication Data
Allen, John L.
     The Kottak anthropology atlas. John L. Allen and Audrey C. Shalinsky.
Guilford, CT: McGraw-Hill/Dushkin, ©2004
56 p.: ill., maps. 21 x 26 cm
I. Anthropology—Atlases. II. Sociology—Atlases. III. Ethnology—Atlases.
     I. Shalinsky, Audrey C.
301
0-07-283228-2

Printed in the United States of America
www.mhhe.com

Contents

About the Authors

John L. Allen is professor and chair of the Department of Geography at the University of Wyoming and emeritus professor of geography at the University of Connecticut, where he taught from 1967 to 2000. He received his bachelor's degree in 1963 and his M.A. in 1964 from the University of Wyoming, and in 1969 his Ph.D. from Clark University. His special areas of interest are perceptions of the environment and the impact of human societies on environmental systems. Dr. Allen is the author and editor of many books and articles as well as several other student atlases, including the best-selling *Student Atlas of World Politics.*

Audrey C. Shalinsky is professor and chair of the Department of Anthropology at the University of Wyoming. She has taught there since 1980. She received her bachelor's degree in 1973 from the University of Chicago and her M.A. and Ph.D. from Harvard University in 1975 and 1979 respectively. A sociocultural anthropologist, Dr. Shalinsky has conducted research in Afghanistan and among Afghan refugees in Pakistan. Her areas of special interest are gender, ethnicity, and the anthropology of religion in the Middle East and South Asia. She has also conducted fieldwork in the United States.

Preface

This atlas is designed to accompany three books by Conrad Phillip Kottak—*Anthropology: The Exploration of Human Diversity* (10th ed.), *Cultural Anthropology* (10th ed.), and *Physical Anthropology and Archaeology*—all published by McGraw-Hill (2004). This atlas allows students to explore the geographic and visual dimensions of anthropology. Since anthropology examines and explains human diversity across space and time, students need help to conceptualize the places and time spans discussed in these textbooks. Where in the world do people live today, and where have they lived at various times in the past?

This atlas, which offers important reference maps to help students, is shrink-wrapped with every copy of each Kottak text. The new "Interpret the World" feature, found in every chapter of all three texts, ties the text to material in the atlas. As they "interpret the world," moving from the text to the atlas, students can see, for example, how the size and shape of the human body vary with mean annual temperature, or how the geographic distribution of human skin color is related to ultraviolet radiation from the sun, or where chiefdoms and states were located in A.D. 1500. Besides the "Interpret the World" feature, new end-of-chapter atlas questions also allow students to draw information from maps, and in some cases, compare different maps to see how information in various chapters is related (for example, the relationship between types of economy [Map 16] and types of political systems [Map 17]).

Introduction: How to Read Maps

An atlas is a book containing maps that are models of the real world. The term *model* means a representation of reality that is generalized, usually considerably smaller than the original, and that emphasizes certain features, depending on the purpose of the model. A model of a car does not contain all of the parts of the original, but it may contain enough parts to be recognizable as a car and may be used to study principles of automotive design or maintenance. A car model designed for racing, on the other hand, may contain fewer parts but would have the mobility of a real automobile. Car models come in a wide variety of types and contain almost anything relative to automobiles that doesn't require the presence of a full-size car. Since anthropologists deal with the real world and its people, virtually all of the printed or published studies in the discipline require models. Unlike a mechanic in an automotive shop, anthropologists can't roll study subjects and their natural settings into the shop to take them apart, study them, and put them back together. They must use models to generalize subjects, and one way to do that is to use maps. Some maps are designed to show specific physical geographic phenomena, such as the topography of the world's surface. Others are intended to portray the distribution of human characteristics across the earth's surface—such as the relative rates of population growth for the world's countries or the distribution of religions. Still other maps may be used to show the relationship between the natural environment and human characteristics—for example, a map of the relationship between human height and weight and the geographic distribution of temperature. Each of these types of maps is found in this atlas. Learning to read and interpret them requires that you understand the following things about maps: (1) that they are made using *projections*; (2) that the maps' level of mathematical proportion, *scale*, affects what you see; and (3) that *generalization* techniques, such as symbols and simplifications, are used where it would be impossible to draw a small version of the real-world feature the map portrays.

MAP PROJECTIONS

Perhaps the most basic problem in *cartography*, or the art and science of mapmaking, is that

Figure 1   The Coordinate System

the subjects of maps—the earth's surface—is what is called by mathematicians "a non-developable surface." Since the world is an approximate sphere (it's actually slightly flattened at the poles and bulges slightly at the equator), it is impossible to flatten out the world or any part of its curved surface without producing some kind of distortion. This "approximate sphere" is represented by a geographic grid, or coordinate system, of latitude lines or *parallels*, that run east and west and measure the north and south distance on the globe and longitude lines, or *meridians,* that run north and south and measure the east and west distance (Figure 1). All the longitude lines are half circles of equal length and converge at the poles. All latitude lines are complete circles that parallel one another and are spaced equidistant on the meridians. The circumference of these circles lessens as you move from the equator. In the real world, all these latitude and longitude grid lines intersect at right angles. The problem for cartographers is to convert this spherical or curved grid into a flat plane. The solution to this problem is the *map projection*—a geometric or mathematical conversion process that translates the sphere to a flat surface. It is important to remember that all projections distort the geographic grid and continental outlines in characteristic ways. The only representation of the world that does not distort either shape or area is a globe. So you can see why we must use projections. Can you imagine carrying an atlas made up entirely of globes back and forth across campus?

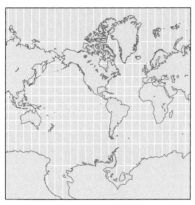

Figure 2 The Mercator Projection

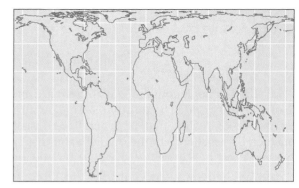

Figure 3 The Peters Projection

It is also important to remember that different projections have been designed for different purposes. The map in Figure 2 is a Mercator projection, named after the famous Dutch cartographer Gerhardus Mercator, who designed the projection in 1567 as a navigation aid. Mercator's projection is unique because all straight lines on the map are lines of constant compass direction in the real world. To lay out a course across the ocean, a navigator could simply draw a straight line between a European port city and one in North America and then keep his ship on course by sailing along the line of constant compass direction. Unfortunately, Mercator's projection, still useful for navigational purposes four and a half centuries after its invention, has been used inappropriately to illustrate things it was never intended to illustrate. The Mercator projection has a tidy rectangular grid that fits the way Europeans and Americans tend to think about space or area. But as the map in Figure 2 shows, it is distorted. It inaccurately shows regions in the higher latitudes (closer to the poles) as larger and mid-latitude and lower-latitude regions as smaller. The projection has often been used incorrectly to show, for example, the countries of the world. So Greenland appears to be larger on the map than South America, when it is actually less than one-seventh the size! This has left generations of school children confused about the real sizes of the countries and many other areal discrepancies.

To make a map that shows regions more accurately in relation to their actual area on the earth's surface, projection techniques other than those used by Mercator need to be used. Unfortunately, many of these projections distort the shapes of countries so badly that the maps end up being funny looking. An example of this kind of map is the recently-developed Peters projection shown in Figure 3. The areas on this map are proportionately correct, but the shapes of the continents are distorted.

Often the solution to the problem of true shape versus true area is resolved by using a compromise projection that shows neither shape nor area in true proportion but gives such a close approximation of each that the world "looks right" and, in fact, the visual impression is much closer to reality. These maps, such as the Robinson projection shown in Figure 4, are often the choice for atlases like this one. But even this projection can present views of the world that may be biased or culturally inappropriate. The Robinson projection in Figure 4 is centered on the Greenwich Prime Meridian, which is the longitude line that runs through the observatory in Greenwich, England. This works nicely for a map intended to show the continental areas of the world. But suppose the primary purpose of the map was to show the Pacific Ocean basin. The map in Figure 4 shows the Pacific is split into eastern and western portions. What would the map look like if the projection were centered in the middle of the Pacific Ocean instead? For an answer, see the map in Figure 5. See how changing the central point of the projections changes your view of the world? The conventional mapping system for global maps is to use the Greenwich Prime Meridian as

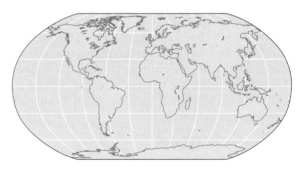

Figure 4 The Robinson Projection

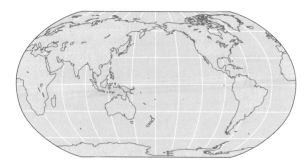

Figure 5   The Robinson Projection centered on 180 degrees

Figure 6   Small-Scale Map of the United States

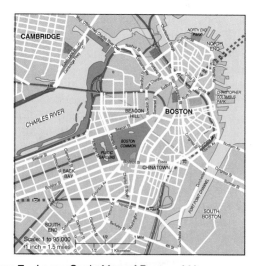

Figure 7   Large-Scale Map of Boston, MA

the center of the map. This allows all continents to be shown without the splitting that would occur if, for example, the central meridian of the map ran through the center of North America. Where a map's central meridian occurs is often a matter of cultural perspective and historical convention. Since so many of our world maps were first drawn in Europe, it was natural that those maps were "Eurocentric." Chinese maps tended to be drawn with China in the center for the same reasons. Most people tend to see their own regions as the most important and, therefore, "central" to maps.

MAP SCALE AND GENERALIZATION

Learning about different projections and how they can distort our worldview is not the only task that students who are interested in understanding how to use an atlas face. They also must understand something about the factor of scale. Since maps are models of the real world, it follows that they are not the same size as the real world or any portion of it. Every map, then, is subject to generalization, which is another way of saying that maps are drawn to certain scales. The only map that would not generalize or simplify would be a map at a scale of 1:1. The term *scale* refers to the mathematical quality of proportional representation, and is expressed as a ratio between an area of the real world or the distance between places on the real world and the same area or distance on the map. You can see why a map at a scale of 1:1 wouldn't be very handy to use since it would be as large as the world itself! The most important thing to keep in mind about scale, and the reason why knowing the map scale is important to reading a map correctly, is the relationship between proportional representation and generalization. A map that fills a page but shows the whole country is much more highly generalized, or *simpler*, than a map that fills a page but shows a single city. On a map of the United States (Figure 6), a city appears

as a dot. On a city map (Figure 7), streets and other features may be clearly seen. When a cartographer simplifies map data, information that is not important for the purposes of the map is just left off. It is important for you to understand that this process of generalization is a subjective one. Depending on the purpose of the map, cartographers will emphasize or deemphasize different features. Often these decisions are made on the basis of cultural or other biases that lend a degree of subjectivity to the map.

Another type of generalization is *classification*. To convey an overall picture of related information, cartographers often group data together in categories. For example, a thematic map showing population growth rates (Figure 8) will use different colors to show groups of growth rates in different classifica-

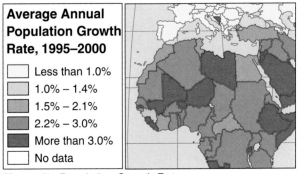

Average Annual Population Growth Rate, 1995–2000

- Less than 1.0%
- 1.0% – 1.4%
- 1.5% – 2.1%
- 2.2% – 3.0%
- More than 3.0%
- No data

Figure 8 Population Growth Rates

tions. Cartographers could never show every single growth rate of every population on one map. Classification is necessary because it is impossible to find enough symbols or colors to represent precise values. Instead, ranges of related information are grouped together. Cartographers show the values of classifications, or the keys to what the classifications mean, in an important section of a map called a legend that make it possible to interpret the patterns shown on the map.

A third generalization technique is *symbolization*. Symbols may include those used to represent cities, as shown in Figures 6 and 7, or the colors used to indicate population growth levels, as shown in Figure 8. Some map symbols are quantitative and show data expressed in mathematical terms such as the rate or percentage of population growth. Other map symbols are qualitative and show data that may be better expressed nonmathematically such as the predominant language or religion of an area. This atlas uses a mixture of quantitative and qualitative symbols to illustrate data of interest to anthropologists. In addition to being quantitative or qualitative, symbols can be classified as "area," "point," or "line" symbols, based on the type of data they represent, a color pattern that shows the rate of population growth for a country is a good example of an area symbol since it covers a certain portion of the earth's surface. Point symbols, such as those used to show the locations of important archaeological sites, show specific locations rather than broad areas, and line symbols showing, for example, the migration of people, plants, and animals, are used to illustrate movement or flow between different points or areas. However they are defined, all symbols are intended to do the same thing: generalize a wide range of very complex data into a form that is readable on a map.

And you thought all you had to do to read an atlas was look at the maps! Now you've learned that it is a bit more involved than that. As you read and study this atlas, keep in mind the principles of projection, scale, and generalization (including simplification, classification, and symbolization) and you'll do just fine. Good luck and enjoy your study of the world of maps as well as maps of the world!

The Kottak

Anthropology Atlas

Map 1 World Topograghy

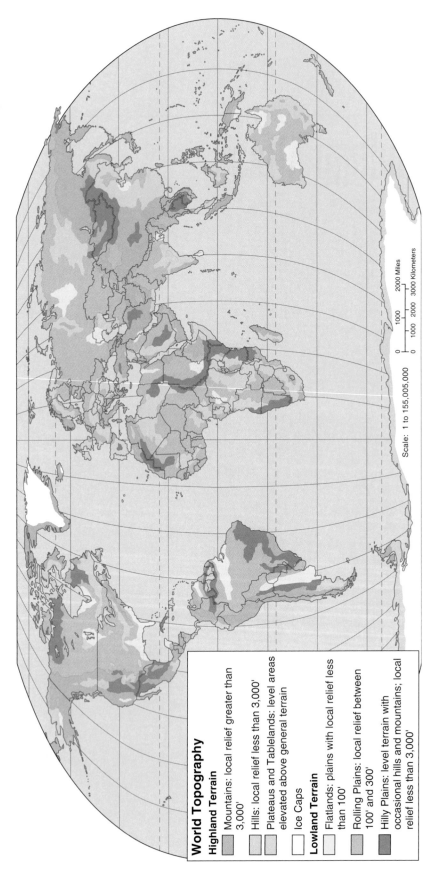

World Topography

Highland Terrain

Mountains: local relief greater than 3,000'

Hills: local relief less than 3,000'

Plateaus and Tablelands: level areas elevated above general terrain

Ice Caps

Lowland Terrain

Flatlands: plains with local relief less than 100'

Rolling Plains: local relief between 100' and 300'

Hilly Plains: level terrain with occasional hills and mountains; local relief less than 3,000'

Scale: 1 to 155,005,000

```
0          1000        2000 Miles
0     1000    2000    3000 Kilometers
```

Topography or terrain, also called "landforms," is second only to climate as a conditioner of human activity, particularly agriculture but also the location of cities and industry. A comparison of this map of mountains, valleys, plains, plateaus, and other features of the earth's surface with a map of land use shows that most of the world's productive agricultural zones are located in lowland and relatively level regions. Where large regions of agricultural productivity are found, we also tend to find urban concentrations and, with cities, we find industry. There is also a good spatial correlation between the map of topography and a map showing the distribution and density of the human population. Normally the world's major landforms are the result of extremely gradual primary geo-logic activity such as the long-term movement of crustal plates. This activity occurs over hundreds of millions of years. Also important is the more rapid (but still slow by human standards) geomorphological or erosional activity of water, wind, glacial ice, and waves, tides, and currents. Some landforms may be produced by abrupt or "cataclysmic" events such as a major volcanic eruption or a meteor strike, but such events are relatively rare and their effects are usually too minor to show up on a map of this scale. The study of the processes that shape topography is known as "geomorphology" and is an important branch of physical geography.

-2-

Map 2 Population Growth Rates

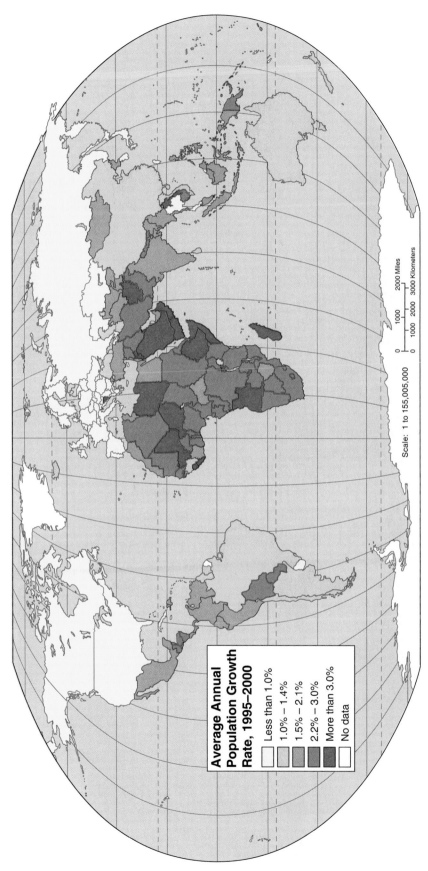

Average Annual Population Growth Rate, 1995–2000

- Less than 1.0%
- 1.0% – 1.4%
- 1.5% – 2.1%
- 2.2% – 3.0%
- More than 3.0%
- No data

Scale: 1 to 155,005,000

0   1000   2000 Miles

0   1000   2000   3000 Kilometers

Of all the statistical measurements of human population, that of the rate of population growth is the most important. The growth rate of a population is a combination of natural change (births and deaths), in-migration, and out-migration; it is obtained by adding the number of births to the number of immigrants during a year and subtracting from that total the sum of deaths and emigrants for the same year. For a specific country, this figure will determine many things about the country's future ability to feed, house, educate, and provide medical services to its citizens. Some of the countries with the largest populations (such as India) also have high growth rates. Since these countries tend to be in developing regions, the combination of high population and high growth rates poses special problems for continuing economic development and carries heightened risks of environmental degradation. Many people believe that the rapidly expanding world population is a potential crisis that may cause environmental and human disaster by the middle of the twenty-first century.

Map 3 Annual Changes in Forest Cover, 1990–1995

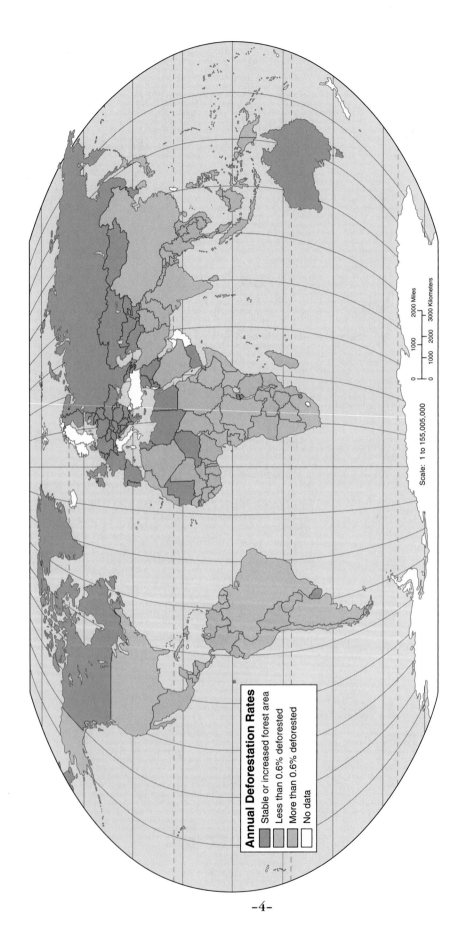

Annual Deforestation Rates

- Stable or increased forest area
- Less than 0.6% deforested
- More than 0.6% deforested
- No data

Scale: 1 to 155,005,000

0   1000   2000 Miles
0   1000   2000   3000 Kilometers

One of the most discussed environmental problems is that of deforestation. For most people, deforestation means clearing of tropical rain forests for agricultural purposes. Yet nearly as much forest land per year—much of it in North America, Europe, and Russia—is impacted by commercial lumbering as is cleared by tropical farmers and ranchers. Even in the tropics, much of the forest clearance is undertaken by large corporations producing high-value tropical hardwoods for the global market in furniture, ornaments, and other fine wood products. Still, it is the agriculturally driven clearing of the great rain forests of the Amazon Basin, west and central Africa, Middle America, and Southeast Asia that draws public attention. Although much concern over forest clearance focuses on the relationship between forest clearance and the reduction in the capacity of the world's vegetation system to absorb carbon dioxide (and thus delay global warming), of just as great concern are issues having to do with the loss of biodiversity (large numbers of plants and animals), the near-total destruction of soil systems, and disruptions in water supply that accompany clearing.

Map 4 Human Variations: Height and Weight

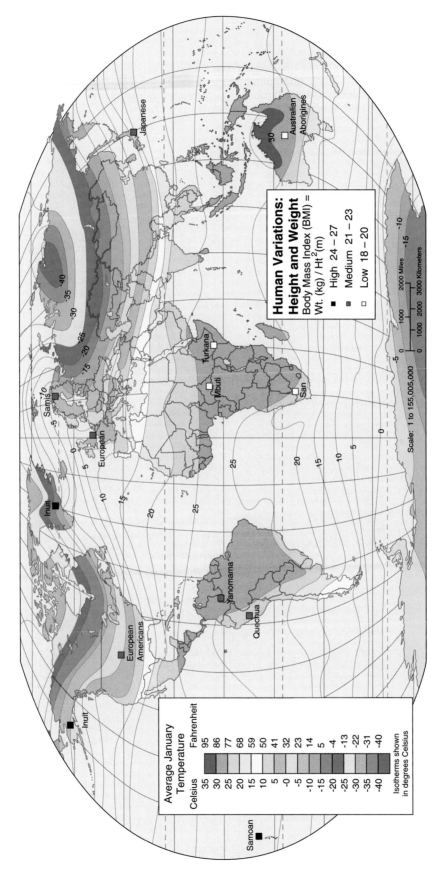

Body Mass Index (BMI), a ratio of height to weight, is determined by a mathematical formula. Most humans have a BMI between 18 and 30. Human groups adapt to their environments biologically and culturally, but biological adaptation is a much slower process. When human groups have been in the same environment for thousands of years, their bodies have adapted biologically to conserve heat or promote cooling.

Map 5 Major Primate Groups

Primates are a zoological order ranging from lemurs to monkeys to apes to humans. With the exception of humans, today primates are found mostly in tropical areas. They used to have a wider distribution, as indicated by places where fossils of ancestral forms have been found.

Major Primate Groups

- Old World and New World Monkeys (living)
- Prosimians (living)
- Apes (living)
- Fossil only

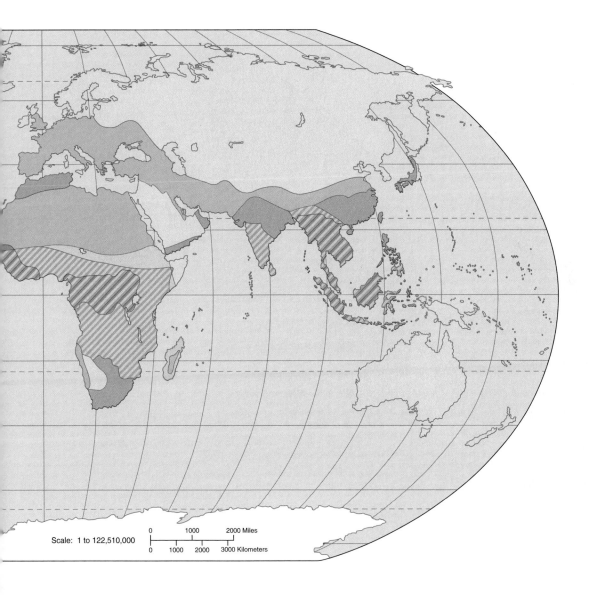

Scale: 1 to 122,510,000

0   1000   2000 Miles

0   1000   2000   3000 Kilometers

Map 6 Evolution of Primates

Scientists trace modern primates back to ancestral forms, just as they do humans. Prosimians, a lower level of primates such as today's lemurs and tarsiers, evolved earliest, almost 60 million years ago, in the Americas. Fossil sites with the ancestors of New World monkeys date back between 23 and 37 million years. Old World monkeys and apes evolved at about the same time, but Old World monkeys spread into many parts of the Old World only in the last 5 million years.

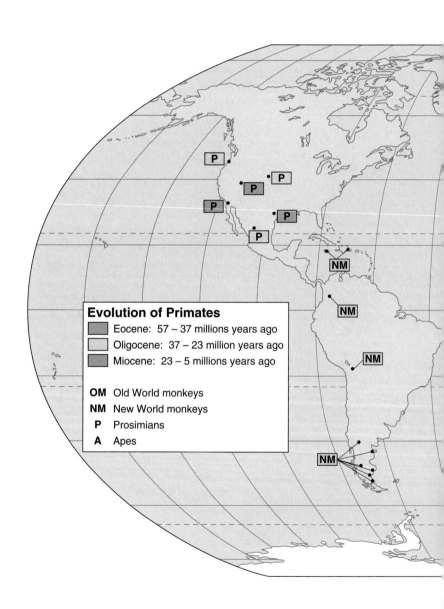

Evolution of Primates

Eocene: 57 – 37 millions years ago
Oligocene: 37 – 23 million years ago
Miocene: 23 – 5 millions years ago

OM Old World monkeys
NM New World monkeys
P Prosimians
A Apes

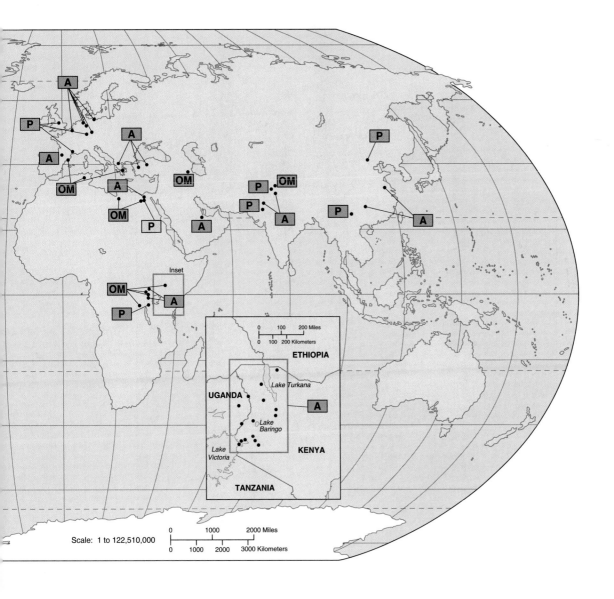

Inset

0   100   200 Miles
0   100   200 Kilometers

ETHIOPIA

UGANDA

Lake Turkana

A

Lake Baringo

Lake Victoria

KENYA

TANZANIA

Scale: 1 to 122,510,000

0   1000   2000 Miles
0   1000   2000   3000 Kilometers

Map 7 Early Hominids: Origins and Diffusion

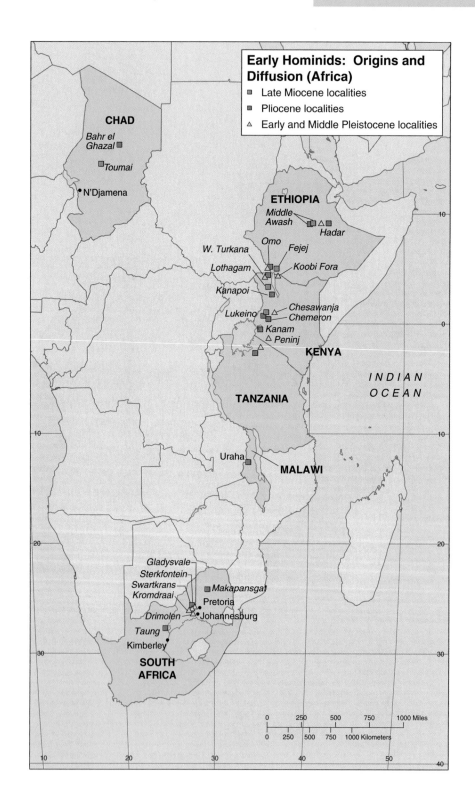

Early Hominids: Origins and Diffusion (Africa)

- ▣ Late Miocene localities
- ▣ Pliocene localities
- △ Early and Middle Pleistocene localities

CHAD

Bahr el Ghazal ▣

▣ Toumai

● N'Djamena

ETHIOPIA

Middle Awash ▣ △ ▣

Hadar

Omo

W. Turkana   Fejej

Lothagam   ▣ Koobi Fora

Kanapoi

Chesawanja

Lukeino   △

Chemeron

▣ Kanam

△ Peninj

KENYA

INDIAN OCEAN

TANZANIA

Uraha ▣

MALAWI

Gladysvale

Sterkfontein

Swartkrans

Kromdraai

▣ Makapansgat

Pretoria ●

Drimolen   ● Johannesburg

Taung ▣

Kimberley ●

SOUTH AFRICA

0   250   500   750   1000 Miles

0   250   500   750   1000 Kilometers

A Time Line of Human Evolution

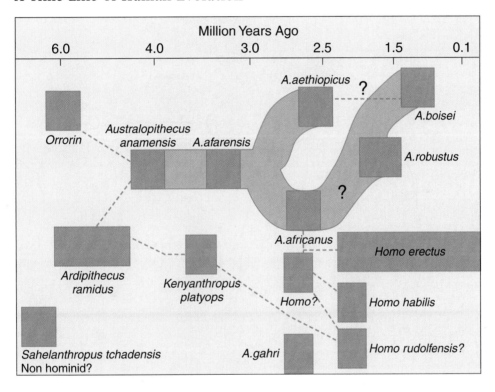

The ancestors of modern humans first evolved in Africa. There are many sites dating to the late Miocene (6–8 million years ago) when the lines leading to modern humans and chimps may first have separated. Scientists agree that in the Pliocene (5–1.8 million years ago), we have sites with the fossil remains of human ancestors, *Homo*. The Pleistocene Era (1.8–10,000 years ago), is the period when humans spread all over the world. Scholars do not always agree on the evolutionary connections between the different fossils, as indicated in the question marks and broken lines on the time line.

Map 8 Origins and Distribution of *Homo sapiens sapiens*

Archaic forms of *Homo sapiens* spread around the world. Modern humans appeared earliest in Africa and migrated into the rest of the Old World between 100,000 and 30,000 years ago. Whether these early modern humans interbred with archaic *Homo sapiens,* including Neandertals, outside of Africa is still debated. Sometime between 9,000 and 25,000 years ago, humans colonized the New World.

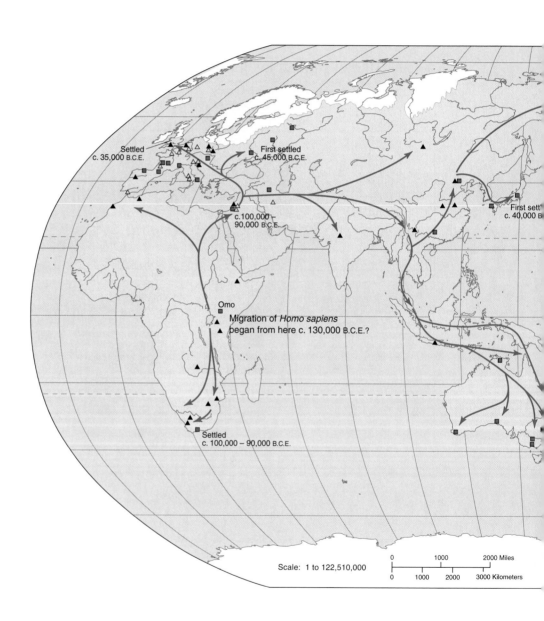

Settled
c. 35,000 B.C.E.

First settled
c. 45,000 B.C.E.

First sett'
c. 40,000 B

c.100,000 –
90,000 B.C.E.

Omo

Migration of *Homo sapiens*
began from here c. 130,000 B.C.E.?

Settled
c. 100,000 – 90,000 B.C.E.

Scale: 1 to 122,510,000

0   1000   2000 Miles

0   1000   2000   3000 Kilometers

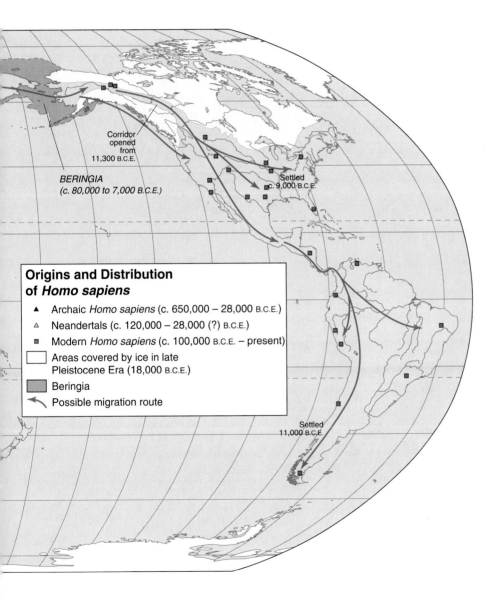

Origins and Distribution of *Homo sapiens*

▲ Archaic *Homo sapiens* (c. 650,000 – 28,000 B.C.E.)
△ Neandertals (c. 120,000 – 28,000 (?) B.C.E.)
■ Modern *Homo sapiens* (c. 100,000 B.C.E. – present)
☐ Areas covered by ice in late Pleistocene Era (18,000 B.C.E.)
▓ Beringia
← Possible migration route

Corridor opened from 11,300 B.C.E.

BERINGIA (c. 80,000 to 7,000 B.C.E.)

Settled c. 9,000 B.C.E.

Settled 11,000 B.C.E.

Map 9 Human Variations: Skin Color

Human skin color varies. The pigmentation is caused by the presence of melanin in the skin, which protects the skin from damage due to ultraviolet radiation. In areas with much UV radiation, people biologically adapted to their environments by increased melanin production.

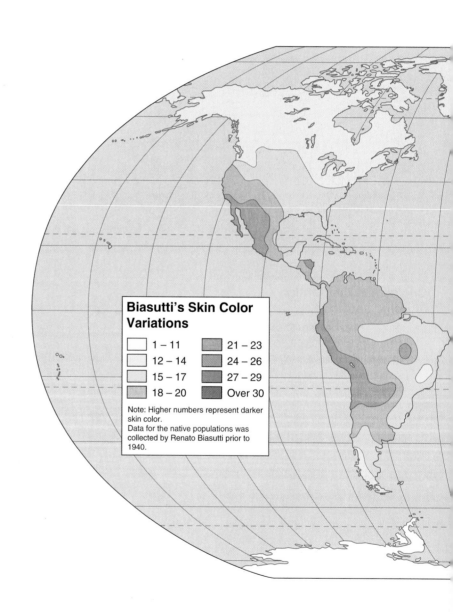

Biasutti's Skin Color Variations

☐	1 – 11	▨	21 – 23
☐	12 – 14	▨	24 – 26
☐	15 – 17	▨	27 – 29
▨	18 – 20	▨	Over 30

Note: Higher numbers represent darker skin color.
Data for the native populations was collected by Renato Biasutti prior to 1940.

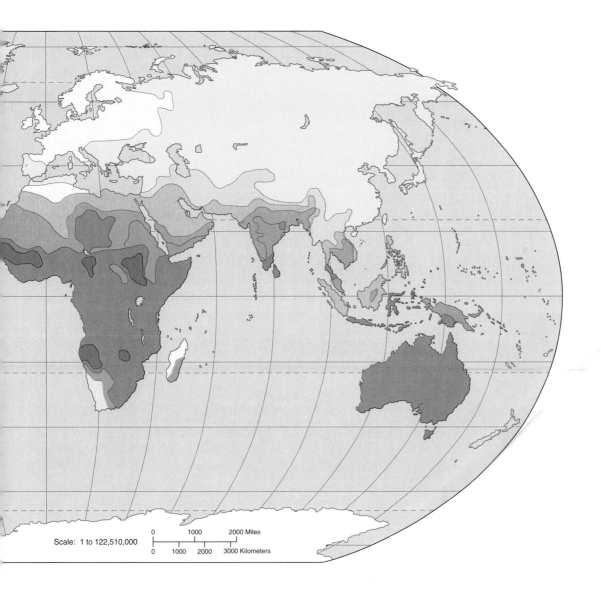

Scale: 1 to 122,510,000

0   1000   2000 Miles

0   1000   2000   3000 Kilometers

Map 10 Early Neolithic Sites of the Middle East and Europe

The Neolithic, or New Stone Age, refers to the period of early farming settlements when people who had been foragers shifted to agriculture. This pattern of subsistence was based on the domestication of plants and animals. Through domestication, people transformed plants

Southwest Asia Domestication

Barley	Goat
Beans	Grapes
Beets	Hemp
Camel	Horse
(Bactrian)	Melons
Carrots	Oats
Cattle	Oil seeds
Dog	Onions
Duck	Rye
Fruits	Sheep
(seed and stone)	Wheat

Mediterranean Domestication

Barley	Goat
Cattle	Grapes
Celery	Lentils
Dates	Lettuce
Garlic	Olives

and animals from their wild state to a form more useful to humans. The Neolithic began in the Fertile Crescent area of the Middle East over 10,000 years ago. It spread to the Levant and Mediterranean, finally reaching Britain and Scandinavia around 5,000 years ago.

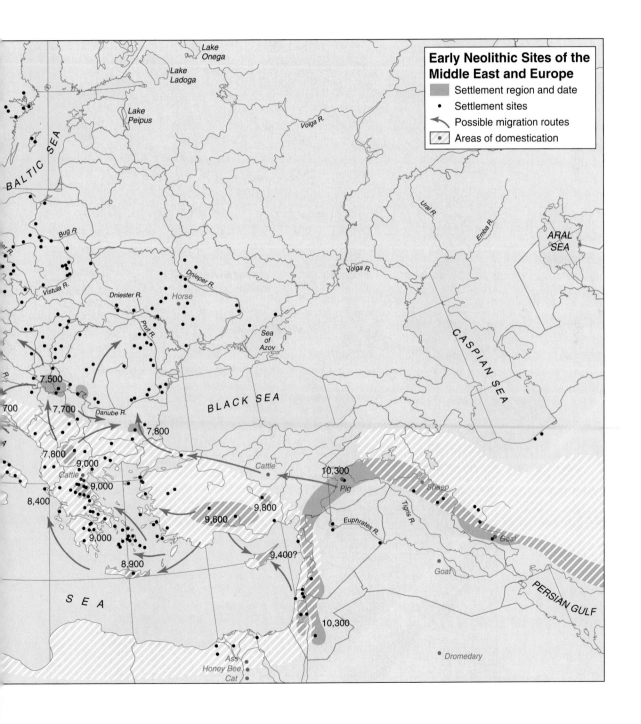

Early Neolithic Sites of the Middle East and Europe

- Settlement region and date
- Settlement sites
- Possible migration routes
- Areas of domestication

Map 11 Ancient Civilizations of the Old World

Archaic states developed in many parts of the Old World at different periods. The earliest civilizations are generally placed at about 3500 B.C.E.

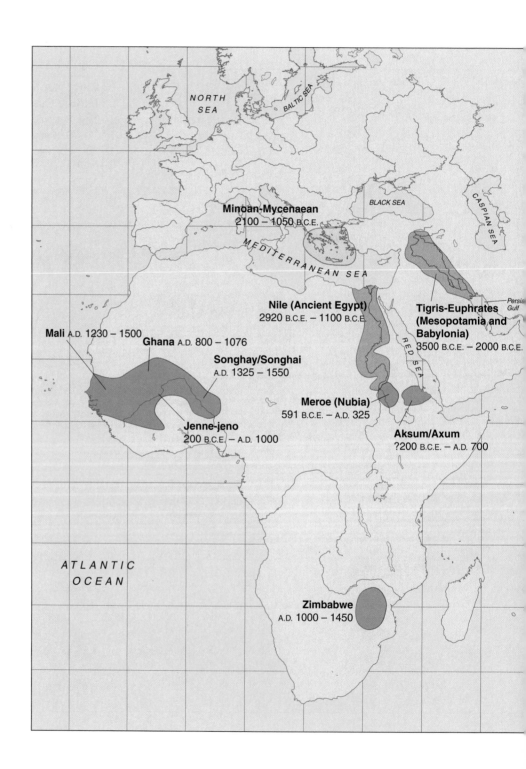

NORTH SEA

BALTIC SEA

BLACK SEA

CASPIAN SEA

Minoan-Mycenaean
2100 – 1050 B.C.E.

MEDITERRANEAN SEA

Persian Gulf

Nile (Ancient Egypt)
2920 B.C.E. – 1100 B.C.E.

Tigris-Euphrates (Mesopotamia and Babylonia)
3500 B.C.E. – 2000 B.C.E.

Mali A.D. 1230 – 1500

Ghana A.D. 800 – 1076

Songhay/Songhai
A.D. 1325 – 1550

RED SEA

Meroe (Nubia)
591 B.C.E. – A.D. 325

Jenne-jeno
200 B.C.E. – A.D. 1000

Aksum/Axum
?200 B.C.E. – A.D. 700

ATLANTIC OCEAN

Zimbabwe
A.D. 1000 – 1450

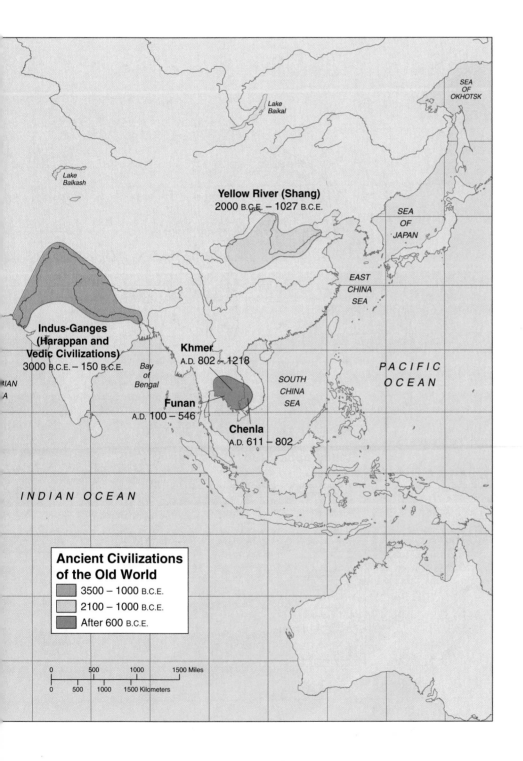

Yellow River (Shang)
2000 B.C.E. – 1027 B.C.E.

Indus-Ganges
(Harappan and
Vedic Civilizations)
3000 B.C.E. – 150 B.C.E.

Khmer
A.D. 802 – 1218

Funan
A.D. 100 – 546

Chenla
A.D. 611 – 802

Lake
Baikal

Lake
Balkash

SEA
OF
OKHOTSK

SEA
OF
JAPAN

EAST
CHINA
SEA

PACIFIC
OCEAN

SOUTH
CHINA
SEA

Bay
of
Bengal

IAN
A

INDIAN OCEAN

**Ancient Civilizations
of the Old World**

  3500 – 1000 B.C.E.
  2100 – 1000 B.C.E.
  After 600 B.C.E.

0   500   1000   1500 Miles

0   500   1000   1500 Kilometers

Map 12 Ethnographic Study Sites Prior to 1950

The modern discipline of anthropology started to develop in the nineteenth century. Field-work in cultural anthropology did not become common practice until the first part of the twentieth century. In the United States, American ethnographers could study Indian people who had been settled on reservations. In England and other European countries, ethnographers often studied those who lived in colonies belonging to the European nation from which the anthropologist had come. Anthropologists frequently studied peoples who were relatively poor and powerless.

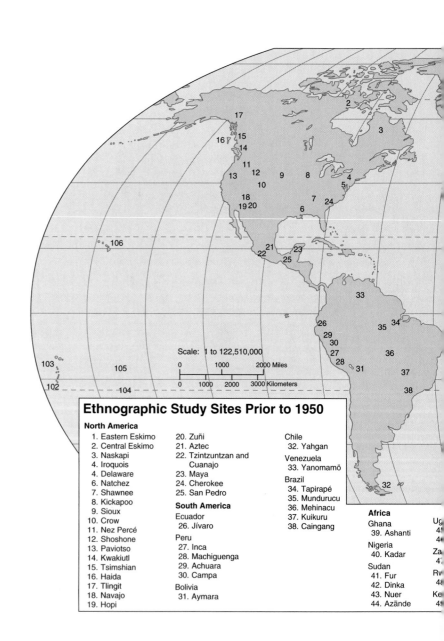

Ethnographic Study Sites Prior to 1950

North America
1. Eastern Eskimo
2. Central Eskimo
3. Naskapi
4. Iroquois
4. Delaware
6. Natchez
7. Shawnee
8. Kickapoo
9. Sioux
10. Crow
11. Nez Percé
12. Shoshone
13. Paviotso
14. Kwakiutl
15. Tsimshian
16. Haida
17. Tlingit
18. Navajo
19. Hopi
20. Zuñi
21. Aztec
22. Tzintzuntzan and Cuanajo
23. Maya
24. Cherokee
25. San Pedro

South America
Ecuador
26. Jívaro
Peru
27. Inca
28. Machiguenga
29. Achuara
30. Campa
Bolivia
31. Aymara
Chile
32. Yahgan
Venezuela
33. Yanomamö
Brazil
34. Tapirapé
35. Mundurucu
36. Mehinacu
37. Kuikuru
38. Caingang

Africa
Ghana
39. Ashanti
Nigeria
40. Kadar
Sudan
41. Fur
42. Dinka
43. Nuer
44. Azãnde

Ug
4
4
Za
4
Rv
4
Ke
4

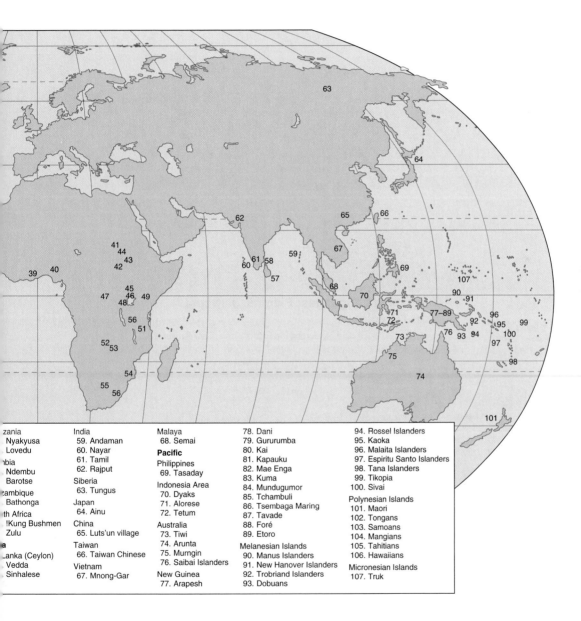

zania	India	Malaya	78. Dani	94. Rossel Islanders
Nyakyusa	59. Andaman	68. Semai	79. Gururumba	95. Kaoka
Lovedu	60. Nayar	**Pacific**	80. Kai	96. Malaita Islanders
nbia	61. Tamil	Philippines	81. Kapauku	97. Espiritu Santo Islanders
Ndembu	62. Rajput	69. Tasaday	82. Mae Enga	98. Tana Islanders
Barotse	Siberia	Indonesia Area	83. Kuma	99. Tikopia
ambique	63. Tungus	70. Dyaks	84. Mundugumor	100. Sivai
Bathonga	Japan	71. Alorese	85. Tchambuli	Polynesian Islands
th Africa	64. Ainu	72. Tetum	86. Tsembaga Maring	101. Maori
!Kung Bushmen	China	Australia	87. Tavade	102. Tongans
Zulu	65. Luts'un village	73. Tiwi	88. Foré	103. Samoans
a	Taiwan	74. Arunta	89. Etoro	104. Mangians
anka (Ceylon)	66. Taiwan Chinese	75. Murngin	Melanesian Islands	105. Tahitians
Vedda	Vietnam	76. Saibai Islanders	90. Manus Islanders	106. Hawaiians
Sinhalese	67. Mnong-Gar	New Guinea	91. New Hanover Islanders	Micronesian Islands
		77. Arapesh	92. Trobriand Islanders	107. Truk
			93. Dobuans	

Map 13 Invented Languages: Pidgins, Jargons, and Creoles

Pidgins are languages that people create when speakers of two different languages have come into contact with each other. They are usually simplified forms that have vocabulary from both languages, which the people use as a second language to be able to talk to members of the other group. Over time, later generations in the area may come to speak this new language as their native tongue. It is then called a creole. Creoles are fully developed grammatical languages. Languages that have developed to meet specialized purposes, such as trade, are known as jargons.

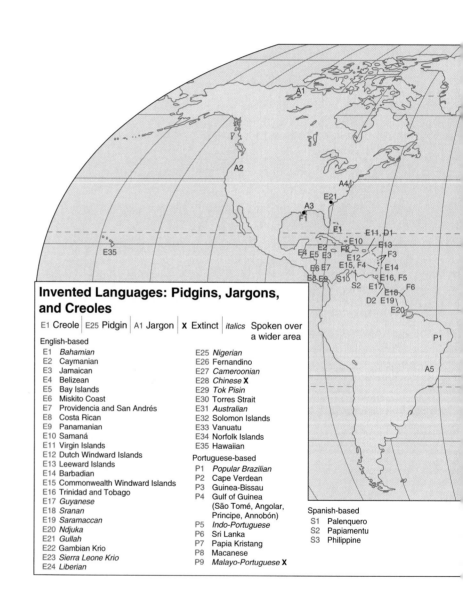

Invented Languages: Pidgins, Jargons, and Creoles

E1 Creole | E25 Pidgin | A1 Jargon | **X** Extinct | *italics* Spoken over a wider area

English-based

E1 *Bahamian*	E25 *Nigerian*
E2 Caymanian	E26 Fernandino
E3 Jamaican	E27 *Cameroonian*
E4 Belizean	E28 *Chinese* **X**
E5 Bay Islands	E29 *Tok Pisin*
E6 Miskito Coast	E30 Torres Strait
E7 Providencia and San Andrés	E31 *Australian*
E8 Costa Rican	E32 Solomon Islands
E9 Panamanian	E33 Vanuatu
E10 Samaná	E34 Norfolk Islands
E11 Virgin Islands	E35 Hawaiian
E12 Dutch Windward Islands	
E13 Leeward Islands	**Portuguese-based**
E14 Barbadian	P1 *Popular Brazilian*
E15 Commonwealth Windward Islands	P2 Cape Verdean
E16 Trinidad and Tobago	P3 Guinea-Bissau
E17 *Guyanese*	P4 Gulf of Guinea
E18 *Sranan*	(São Tomé, Angolar,
E19 *Saramaccan*	Principe, Annobón)
E20 *Ndjuka*	P5 *Indo-Portuguese*
E21 *Gullah*	P6 Sri Lanka
E22 Gambian Krio	P7 Papia Kristang
E23 *Sierra Leone Krio*	P8 Macanese
E24 *Liberian*	P9 *Malayo-Portuguese* **X**

Spanish-based

S1 Palenquero
S2 Papiamentu
S3 Philippine

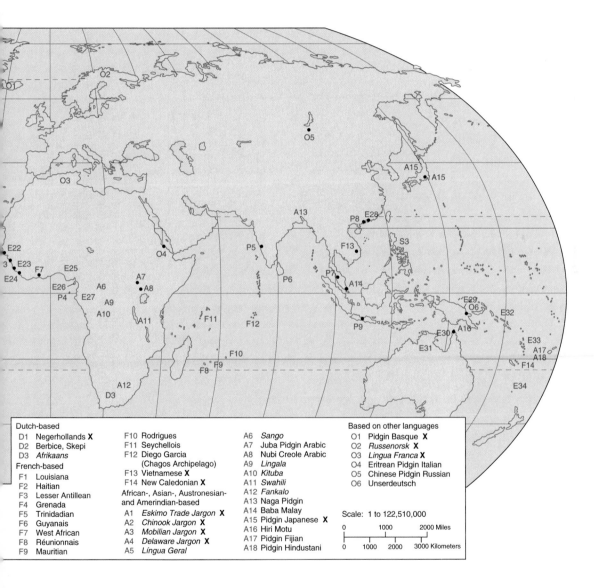

Dutch-based
D1 Negerhollands **X**
D2 Berbice, Skepi
D3 *Afrikaans*

French-based
F1 Louisiana
F2 Haitian
F3 Lesser Antillean
F4 Grenada
F5 Trinidadian
F6 Guyanais
F7 West African
F8 Réunionnais
F9 Mauritian

F10 Rodrigues
F11 Seychellois
F12 Diego Garcia
     (Chagos Archipelago)
F13 Vietnamese **X**
F14 New Caledonian **X**

African-, Asian-, Austronesian-
and Amerindian-based
A1 *Eskimo Trade Jargon* **X**
A2 *Chinook Jargon* **X**
A3 *Mobilian Jargon* **X**
A4 *Delaware Jargon* **X**
A5 *Língua Geral*

A6 *Sango*
A7 Juba Pidgin Arabic
A8 Nubi Creole Arabic
A9 *Lingala*
A10 *Kituba*
A11 *Swahili*
A12 *Fankalo*
A13 Naga Pidgin
A14 Baba Malay
A15 Pidgin Japanese **X**
A16 Hiri Motu
A17 Pidgin Fijian
A18 Pidgin Hindustani

Based on other languages
O1 Pidgin Basque **X**
O2 *Russenorsk* **X**
O3 *Lingua Franca* **X**
O4 Eritrean Pidgin Italian
O5 Chinese Pidgin Russian
O6 Unserdeutsch

Scale: 1 to 122,510,000

0 · · · 1000 · · · 2000 Miles

0 · · · 1000 · · · 2000 · · · 3000 Kilometers

Map 14 Global Distribution of Minority Groups

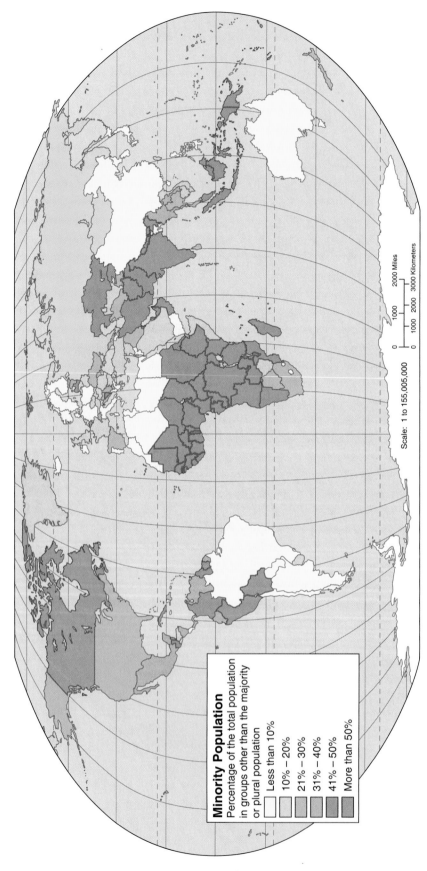

Minority Population

Percentage of the total population in groups other than the majority or plural population

- Less than 10%
- 10% – 20%
- 21% – 30%
- 31% – 40%
- 41% – 50%
- More than 50%

Scale: 1 to 155,005,000

0   1000   2000 Miles

0   1000   2000   3000 Kilometers

The presence of minority ethnic, national, or racial groups within a country's population can add a vibrant and dynamic mix to the whole. Plural societies with a high degree of cultural and ethnic diversity should, according to some social theorists, be among the world's most healthy. Unfortunately, the reality of the situation is quite different from theory or expectation. The presence of significant minority populations played an important role in the disintegration of the Soviet Union, and the continuing existence of minority populations within the former Soviet republics threatened the viability and stability of those young political units. In Africa, national boundaries were drawn by colonial powers without regard for the geographical distribution of ethnic groups, and the continuing tribal conflicts that have resulted hamper both economic and political development.

Map 15 World Languages

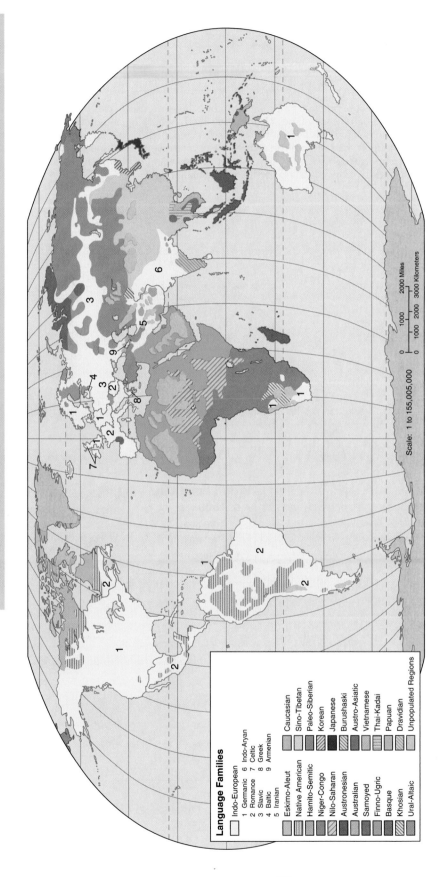

Language Families

Indo-European
1 Germanic 6 Indo-Aryan
2 Romance   7 Celtic
3 Slavic   8 Greek
4 Baltic   9 Armenian
5 Iranian

Eskimo-Aleut
Native American
Hamito-Semitic
Niger-Congo
Nilo-Saharan
Austronesian
Australian
Samoyed
Finno-Ugric
Basque
Khoisan
Ural-Altaic

Caucasian
Sino-Tibetan
Paleo-Siberian
Korean
Japanese
Burushaski
Austro-Asiatic
Vietnamese
Thai-Kadai
Papuan
Dravidian
Unpopulated Regions

Scale: 1 to 155,005,000

0   1000   2000 Miles
0 1000 2000 3000 Kilometers

Language, like religion, is an important identifying characteristic of culture. Indeed, it is perhaps the most durable of all other identifying characteristics or cultural traits, such as religion, institutions, material technologies, and ways of making a living. After centuries of exposure to other languages or even conquest by speakers of other languages, the speakers of a specific tongue will often retain their own linguistic identity. As a geographic element, language helps us to locate areas of potential conflict, particularly in regions where two or more languages overlap. Many, if not most, of the world's conflict zones are also areas of linguistic diversity and knowing the distribution of languages helps us to understand some of the reasons behind important current events; for example,

linguistic identity differences played an important part in the disintegration of the Soviet Union in the early 1990s; and in areas emerging from recent colonial rule, such as Africa, the participants in conflicts over territory and power are often defined in terms of linguistic groups. Language distributions also help us to comprehend the nature of the human past by providing clues that enable us to chart the course of human migrations, as shown in the distribution of Indo-European, Austronesian, or Hamito-Semitic languages. Finally, because languages have a great deal to do with the way people perceive and understand the world around them, linguistic patterns help to explain the global variations in the ways that people interact with their environments.

-25-

Map 16   World Land Use, A.D. 1500

Europeans began to explore the world in the late 1400s. They encountered many indepen-
dent people with self-sustaining economies at that time. Foraging people practiced hunting
and gathering, utilizing the wild forms of plants and animals in their environments. Horti-
cultural people practiced a simple form of cultivation using hoes or digging sticks as their
basic tools. They sometimes cleared their land by burning and then planted crops. Pasto-
ralists herded animals as their basic subsistence pattern. Some state-level societies, such as
the Mongols, had pastoralism as their base. Intensive agriculturalists based their societies
on complicated irrigation systems and/or the plow and draft animals. Wheat and rice were
two kinds of crops that supported large populations.

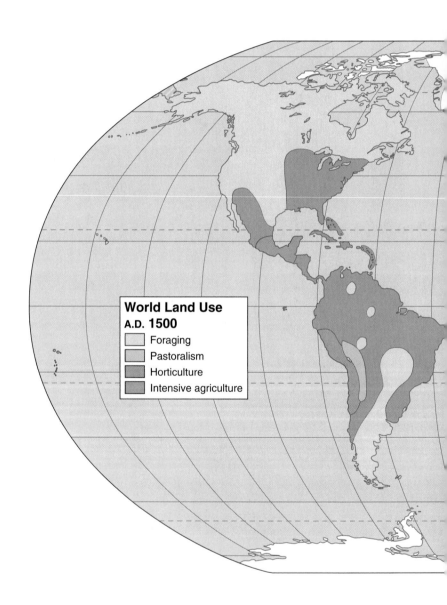

World Land Use
A.D. 1500
Foraging
Pastoralism
Horticulture
Intensive agriculture

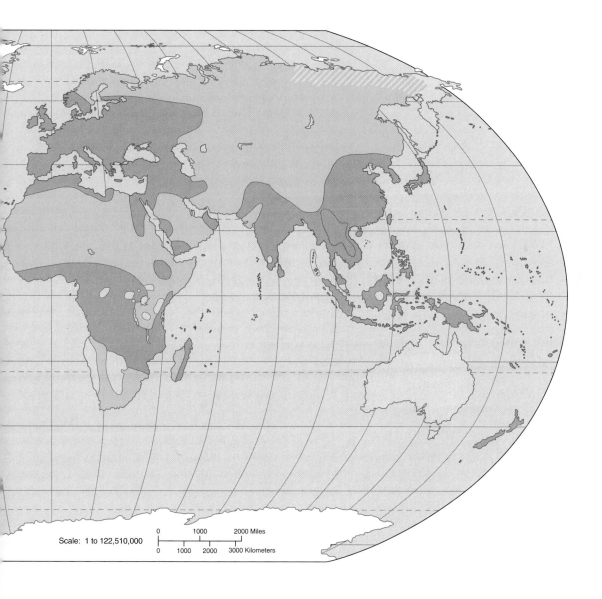

Scale: 1 to 122,510,000

0		1000		2000 Miles
0	1000	2000	3000 Kilometers

Map 17 Organized States and Chiefdoms, A.D. 1500

When the Europeans began to explore the world in the fifteenth through seventeenth centuries, they found complex political organizations in many places. Both chiefdoms and states are large-scale forms of political organization in which some people have privileged access to power, wealth, and prestige. Chiefdoms are kin-based societies in which redistribution is the major economic pattern. States are organized in terms of socioeconomic classes, headed by a centralized government that is led by an elite. States include a full-time bureaucracy and specialized subsystems for such activities as military action, taxation, and social control.

ATLANTIC OCEAN

PACIFIC OCEAN

TARASCA

AZTEC STATE

OTHER MEXICAN STATES

CHIBCHA

Organized States and Chiefdoms, A.D. 1500

- No chiefdoms or states
- Chiefdoms
- OYO States

INCA STATE

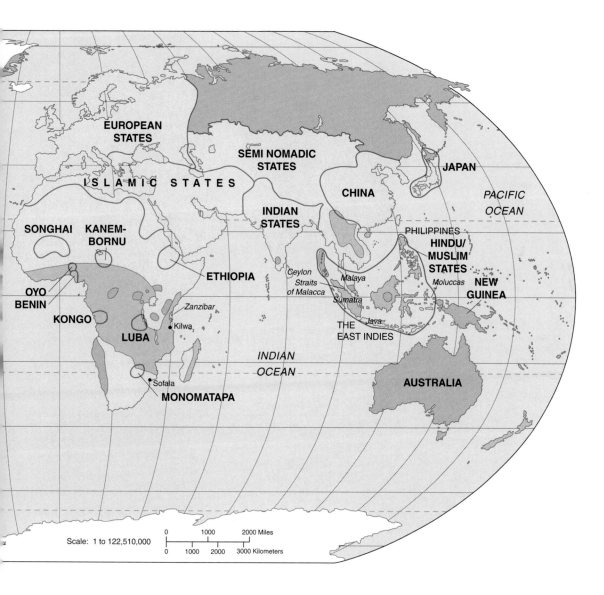

EUROPEAN STATES

SEMI NOMADIC STATES

JAPAN

ISLAMIC STATES

CHINA

PACIFIC OCEAN

SONGHAI

KANEM-BORNU

INDIAN STATES

PHILIPPINES

HINDU/ MUSLIM STATES

ETHIOPIA

OYO BENIN

Ceylon
Straits of Malacca

Malaya

Moluccas

NEW GUINEA

KONGO

Zanzibar

Sumatra

LUBA

Kilwa

THE EAST INDIES

Java

INDIAN OCEAN

Sofala

MONOMATAPA

AUSTRALIA

Scale: 1 to 122,510,000

0   1000   2000 Miles

0   1000   2000   3000 Kilometers

Map 18 Household and Family Structures

Nuclear families are composed of a married couple and their children. They are found all over the world in many different kinds of cultural systems. Foraging peoples and industrial people find that nuclear families make for efficient and mobile households. Even when different forms of households are preferred in a society, nuclear families may still exist. For example, in traditional intensive agricultural societies, like India, people found it useful to live in larger households in which three generations—the grandparents, their married sons and their wives, and their children—all resided together and shared the work. When the

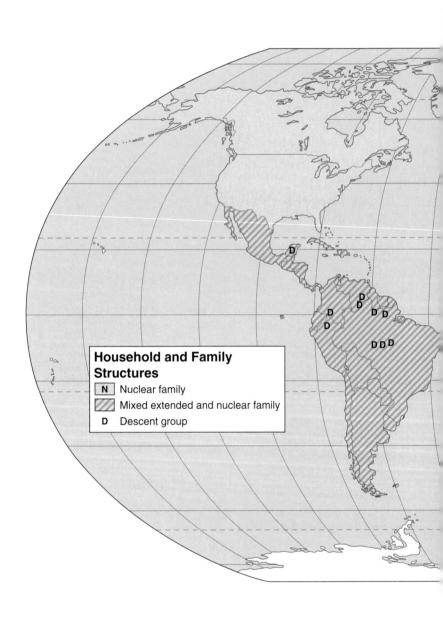

Household and Family Structures

N	Nuclear family
	Mixed extended and nuclear family
D	Descent group

oldest generation died, however, the sons sometimes divided the household and thus lived in nuclear families. Descent groups, such as lineages or clans, are a different sort of social structural unit that exists in perpetuity. Descent groups often own land or herds in common and assign labor to subunits. They are common in tribal societies in which horticulture or pastoralism is practiced. The map provides an overview of the last 100 years of typical household patterns.

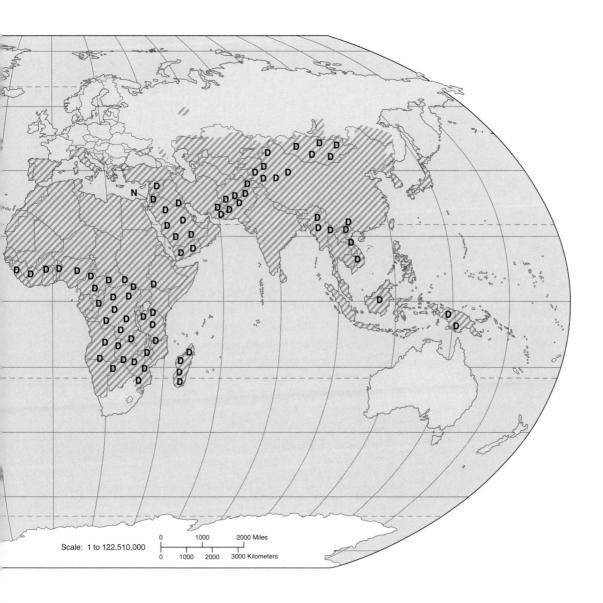

Map 19 Systems of Marriage Relationships

Monogamy, in which a person has only one spouse at a time, is a common form of marriage. Monogamy is found all over the world even though it is not always the preferred form of marriage. Polygyny, a man married to two or more women at the same time, has traditionally been allowed and even favored in many parts of the world. Often, however, only wealthy and powerful men can afford more than one wife. Polyandry, a woman married to

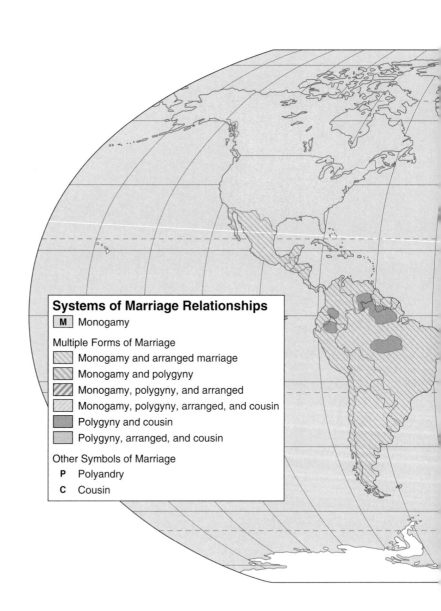

Systems of Marriage Relationships

| M | Monogamy |

Multiple Forms of Marriage

- Monogamy and arranged marriage
- Monogamy and polygyny
- Monogamy, polygyny, and arranged
- Monogamy, polygyny, arranged, and cousin
- Polygyny and cousin
- Polygyny, arranged, and cousin

Other Symbols of Marriage

- **P** Polyandry
- **C** Cousin

two or men at the same time, is very rare and is found in some parts of South Asia. Marriage has not usually been an individual's choice. In much of the world, families play an important role in arranging marriages. In tribal societies, it is often considered most appropriate to marry someone who is classified as a cross or parallel cousin. The map provides an overview of the last 100 years of traditional marriage patterns and preferences.

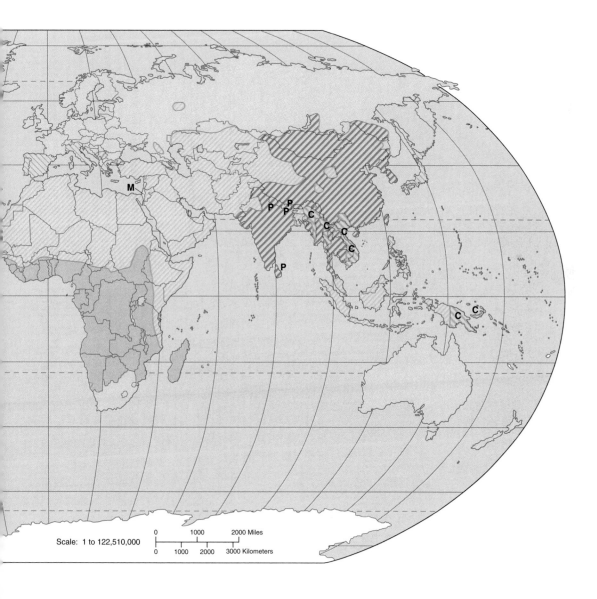

Map 20 Female/Male Inequality in Education and Employment

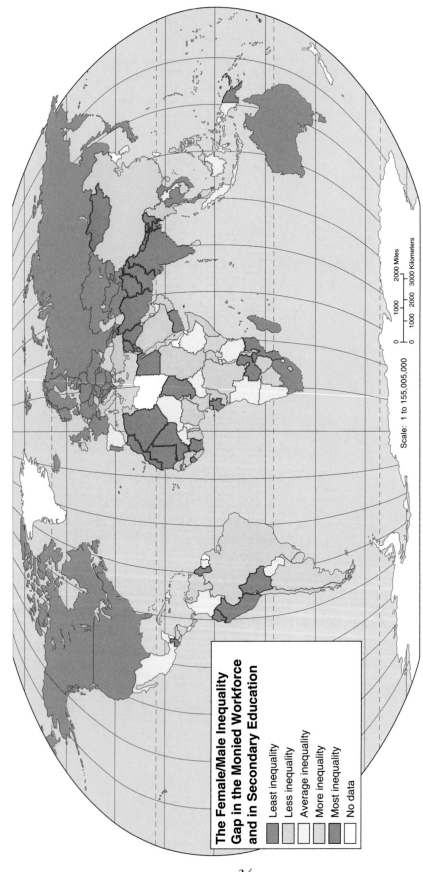

The Female/Male Inequality
Gap in the Monied Workforce
and in Secondary Education

- Least inequality
- Less inequality
- Average inequality
- More inequality
- Most inequality
- No data

Scale: 1 to 155,005,000

0   1000   2000 Miles

0 1000 2000 3000 Kilometers

While women in developed countries, particularly in North America and Europe, have made significant advances in socioeconomic status in recent years, in most of the world females suffer from significant inequality when compared with their male counterparts. Although women have received the right to vote in most of the world's countries, in over 90 percent of these countries that right has only been granted in the last 50 years. In most regions, literacy rates for women still fall far short of those for men; In Africa and Asia, for example, only about half as many women are as literate as men. Women marry considerably younger than men and attend school for shorter periods of time. Inequalities in education and employment are perhaps the most telling indicators of the unequal status of women in most of the world. Lack of secondary education in comparison with men prevents women from entering the workforce with equally high-paying jobs. Even where women are employed in positions similar to those held by men, they still tend to receive less compensation. The gap between rich and poor involves not only a clear geographic differentiation, but a clear gender differentiation as well.

Map 21 World Religions

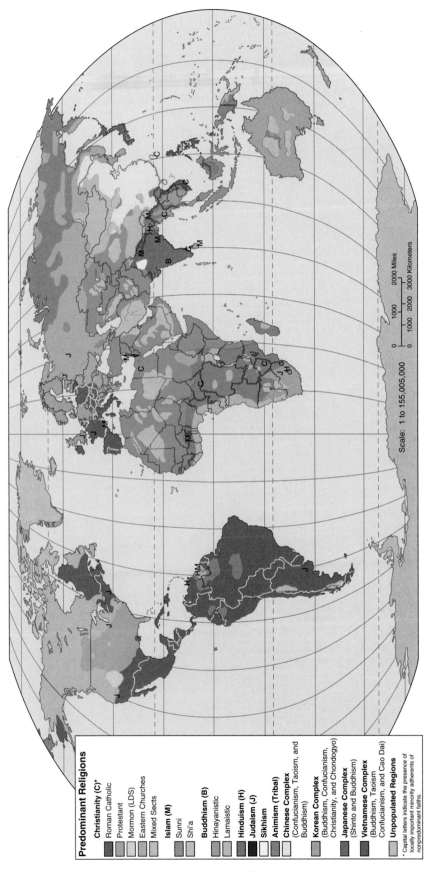

Predominant Religions

Christianity (C)*
- Roman Catholic
- Protestant
- Mormon (LDS)
- Eastern Churches
- Mixed Sects

Islam (M)
- Sunni
- Shi'a

Buddhism (B)
- Hinayanistic
- Lamaistic

Hinduism (H)

Judaism (J)

Sikhism

Animism (Tribal)

Chinese Complex
(Confucianism, Taoism, and Buddhism)

Korean Complex
(Buddhism, Confucianism, Christianity, and Chondogyo)

Japanese Complex
(Shinto and Buddhism)

Vietnamese Complex
(Buddhism, Taoism Confucianism, and Cao Dai)

Unpopulated Regions

* Capital letters indicate the presence of locally important minority adherents of nonpredominant faiths.

Scale: 1 to 155,005,000

0   1000   2000 Miles

0   1000 2000 3000 Kilometers

Religious adherence is one of the fundamental defining characteristics of human culture, the style of life adopted by a people and passed from one generation to the next. Because of the importance of religion for culture, a depiction of the spatial distribution of religions is as close as we can come to a map of cultural patterns. More than just a set of behavioral patterns having to do with worship and ceremony, religion is a vital conditioner of the ways that people deal with one another, with their institutions, and with the environments they occupy. In many areas of the world, the ways in which people make a living, the patterns of occupation that they create on the land, and the impacts that they make on ecosystems are the direct consequences of their adherence to a religious faith. An examination of the map in the context of international and intra-national conflict will show that tension between countries and the internal stability of states is also a function of the spatial distribution of religion.

Map 22 Megaliths, Petroglyphs, and Cave Paintings

Some examples of ancient art are petroglyphs (rock carvings), pictographs (designs pecked into rock), cave paintings, and megaliths (architectural stone features built on the landscape).

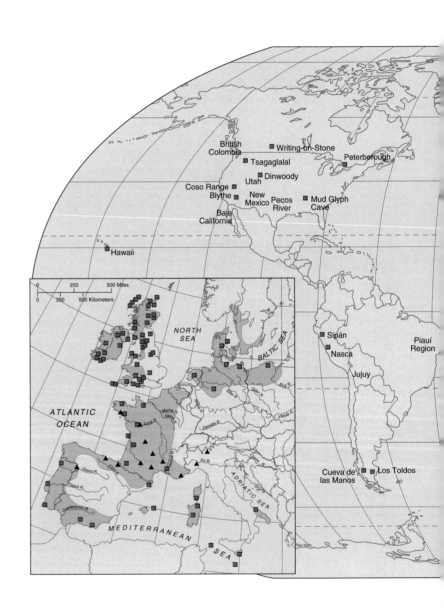

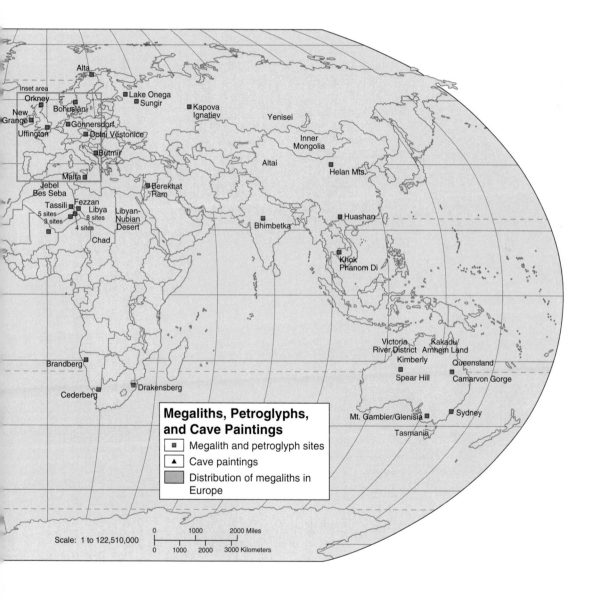

Alta

Inset area
Orkney
Lake Onega
New
Grange
Bohuslän
Sungir
Kapova
Ignatiev
Yenisei
Göhnersdorf
Uffington
Dolni Věstonice
Inner
Mongolia
Butmir
Altai
Helan Mts.
Malta
Berekhat
Ram
Jebel
Bes Seba
Fezzan
Tassili
Libya
5 sites
8 sites
Libyan-
Nubian
Desert
Bhimbetka
Huashan
3 sites
4 sites
Chad
Khok
Phanom Di

Brandberg
Victoria
River District
Kakadu/
Arnhem Land
Kimberly
Queensland
Cederberg
Drakensberg
Spear Hill
Camarvon Gorge
Mt. Gambier/Glenisia
Sydney
Tasmania

**Megaliths, Petroglyphs,
and Cave Paintings**

■ Megalith and petroglyph sites

▲ Cave paintings

▨ Distribution of megaliths in
Europe

Scale: 1 to 122,510,000

0   1000   2000 Miles

0   1000   2000   3000 Kilometers

Map 23 Energy Consumption Per Capita

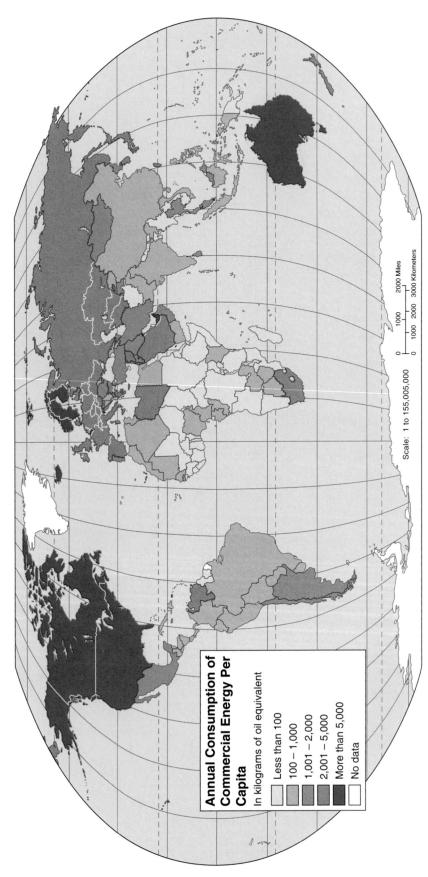

Annual Consumption of Commercial Energy Per Capita

In kilograms of oil equivalent

- Less than 100
- 100 – 1,000
- 1,001 – 2,000
- 2,001 – 5,000
- More than 5,000
- No data

Scale: 1 to 155,005,000

```
0              1000            2000 Miles
0       1000    2000    3000 Kilometers
```

Of all the quantitative measures of economic well-being, energy consumption per capita may be the most expressive. All of the countries defined by the World Bank as having high incomes consume at least 100 gigajoules of commercial energy (the equivalent of about 3.5 metric tons of coal) per person per year, with some, such as the United States and Canada, having consumption rates in the 300 gigajoule range (the equivalent of more than 10 metric tons of coal per person per year). With the exception of the oil-rich Persian Gulf states, where consumption figures include the costly "burning off" of excess energy in the form of natural gas flares at wellheads, most of the highest-consuming countries are in the Northern Hemisphere, concentrated in North America and Western Europe. At the other end of the scale are low-income countries, whose consumption rates are often less than 1 percent of those of the United States and other high consumers. These figures do not, of course, include the consumption of non-commercial energy—the traditional fuels of firewood, animal dung, and other organic matter—widely used in the less developed parts of the world.

Map 24 The Quality of Life: The Index of Human Development

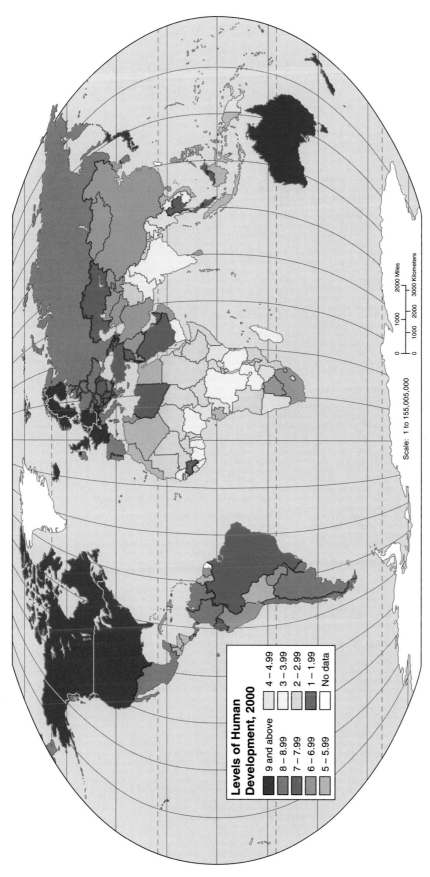

Levels of Human Development, 2000

- 9 and above
- 8 – 8.99
- 7 – 7.99
- 6 – 6.99
- 5 – 5.99
- 4 – 4.99
- 3 – 3.99
- 2 – 2.99
- 1 – 1.99
- No data

Scale: 1 to 155,005,000

0   1000   2000 Miles
0 1000 2000 3000 Kilometers

The development index upon which this map is based takes into account a wide variety of demographic, health, and educational data, including population growth, per capita gross domestic income, longevity, literacy, and years of schooling. The map reveals significant improvement in the quality of life in Middle and South America, although it is questionable whether the gains made in those regions can be maintained in the face of the dramatic population increases expected over the next 30 years. More clearly than anything else, the map illustrates the near-desperate situation in Africa and South Asia. In those regions, the unparalleled growth in population threatens to overwhelm all

efforts to improve the quality of life. In Africa, for example, the population is increasing by 20 million persons per year. With nearly 45 percent of the continent's population aged 15 years or younger, this growth rate will accelerate as the women reach childbearing age. Africa, along with South Asia, faces the very difficult challenge of providing basic access to health care, education, and jobs for a rapidly increasing population. The map also illustrates the striking difference in quality of life between those who inhabit the world's equatorial and tropical regions and those fortunate enough to live in the temperate zones, regions, where the quality of life is significantly higher.

Map **25**   Indigenous Peoples of the World, 2000

Indigenous peoples are not only those who are born and live in a particular place; indigenous peoples are the descendants of the first inhabitants of that area. Today these peoples are arguing for their land and political rights, which have often been diminished as other groups have taken control of their economies.

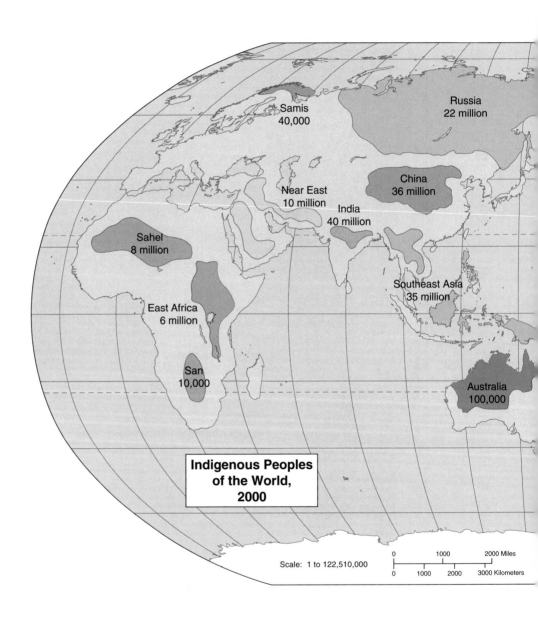

Indigenous Peoples of the World, 2000

Samis
40,000

Russia
22 million

Near East
10 million

China
36 million

India
40 million

Sahel
8 million

Southeast Asia
35 million

East Africa
6 million

San
10,000

Australia
100,000

Scale: 1 to 122,510,000

0   1000   2000 Miles

0   1000   2000   3000 Kilometers